THE CRY OF A PROPHETESS

BY

LASHANDA WILLIAMS

Copyright © 2015 by Lashanda Williams

The Cry Of A Prophetess
by Lashanda Williams

Printed in the United States of America.

ISBN 9781498449090

All rights reserved solely by the author. The author guarantees all contents are original and do not infringe upon the legal rights of any other person or work. No part of this book may be reproduced in any form without the permission of the author. The views expressed in this book are not necessarily those of the publisher.

Scripture quotations taken from The Scofield Study Bible. Copyright © 2006 by Oxford University Press. Used by permission. All rights reserved.

Scripture quotations taken from the King James Version (KJV) – public domain

www.xulonpress.com

TABLE OF CONTENTS

The Call: Chosen 7
The Making 11
The Cry 15
The Beginning Of Life 19
New Life In Christ 23
Trusting Christ Despite Life's Trials 27
Order Of Mankind 33
Personal Testimony Of Marriage And Submission 35
The Order Of God. 39

Chapter 1:

THE CALL: CHOSEN

Our purpose on earth is not to get lost in the dark in our journey through life's trials, but to be a beacon of light so others, too, may find their way. Beacon is a strong light that can be seen afar for guidance. I know that everything that happened in my life was for a purpose and reason. I received my calling into the ministry in 2004. I always felt the hand of God in my life as young girl, but I didn't understand what it was. I would dream things, and they would happen *exactly* the way I dreamed them. I would think something in my mind and whatever I thought would happen. As a young lady, I thought I was strange. I would always speak my mind and truth. I did not compromise for nothing or nobody. The devil tried to destroy me in my mother's womb. He knew if I gave my life to the Lord and I discovered who I really was in Christ, God would use me to speak to nations and people would be healed, delivered and freed. The devil knew I would tear down his kingdom.

To God be the glory, the Lord has placed a holy boldness inside of me, giving my testimony, and telling of God's goodness and what He expects out of His people. This is something I live to do. No matter what people may say about me, I will still stand on God's word. I will give Him praise, preach and teach what the Lord leads me to say regardless of how people feel or think. *Luke 1:71-79* Authorized King James Version, Thomas Nelson, Inc. tells us,

> That I should be saved from my enemies, and from the hand of all that hate me; to perform the mercy promised to our fathers, and remember His holy covenant; the oath which God swear to Abraham, our father of many nations, that we being delivered out the hand of our enemies might serve God without fear; And thou, child, shall be called the prophet of the Highest: for thou shall go before the face the Lord to prepare his ways; to give knowledge of salvation unto His people by remission of their sins; to give light to them that sit in darkness and in the shadow of death, to guide feet unto the way of peace.

Isaiah 61:1-3 Authorized King James Version, Thomas Nelson, Inc. also tells us,

> The Spirit of the Lord God is upon me; because the Lord has anointed me to preach good tidings unto the meek; he hath sent me to bind up the brokenhearted, to proclaim liberty to the captives, and the opening of the prison to them that are bound; to proclaim the acceptable year of the Lord, and the day of vengeance of our God; to comfort all that mourn; to appoint unto them that mourn in Zion, to give them beauty for ashes, the oil of joy for mourning, the garment of praise for the spirit of heaviness; that might be called trees of righteousness, the planting of the Lord, that he might be glorified.

My whole life has been torment and hell. I remember growing up hating that I was born and wondering why. As I got older, I felt confused and self-conscious. I knew I was different and I didn't understand what I saw and heard, nor did I have anyone to talk to or help me. In 1999, I got saved and filled with the Holy Spirit. Wow, that was the best to ever happened to me. I went full force in seeking the kingdom of God through prayer, fasting, and studying the word of God.

I started as an usher but I knew my calling was higher. In 2004, I was asleep and the Holy Spirit spoke to me in a dream. In this dream, I was on a fish bank and the water was more like and ocean rather than a lake. A voice spoke to me and said, "Throw your line into the ocean." I did as the voice commanded me and when I pulled the line out, it was a small fish at the end of it. The voice said, "Take that fish off and throw it deeper into the sea." Again, I did as I was commanded and I slung the fishing reel with much strength as I could. This time, my line was about to break, who when I pulled it up, a big fish was on the hook. The Holy Spirit spoke to me and said, "Daughter, I have chosen you, I chose you before your were formed in your mother's womb. I called you to be my evangelist, and not only evangelist but you shall also be my end time prophetess. I will use our mouthpiece to speak to the nations. Those who take heed and hear the warnings and the word spoken through you will be blessed. Those who reject you will be damned (cursed)!!!!! They are not rejecting you but they're rejecting me.

***He that receiveth a prophet in the name of a prophet
shall receive a prophet's reward, Matthew 10:41.***

Prophetess comes from the Hebrew word *neviah*. The Greek word is propheti which means speak before. A prophetess is a woman who exercised in the prophetic gift in ancient Israel or in the early Christian Church (All-in-One Bible Reference Guide, Zondervan, 2008).

Prophet means speak before, also. Three Hebrew word are used in the Old Testament to designate the prophets. They were navi, roeh, and hozeh. Prophets were called "seers." Prophets are the ones who speak from God (All-in-One Bible Reference Guide, Zondervan, 2008).

THE MAKING

Once I accepted my calling, the spiritual battle began. I would attend church and the Holy Spirit would begin to speak through me and people would get offended. No matter what I said or where I went, I would start getting lashes from the pulpit. I was like Lord, I say what you want me to tell the people and they take it as being harsh and unloving. Some even would take it personal and say I was talking about them. Wow, I really didn't understand what was going on. I felt like Jeremiah. Every time I opened my mouth I was attacked. But I couldn't shut my mouth. It was like fire shut up in my bones. I would literally sweat and I had to open my mouth and speak. If I had not, I would feel convicted and I would be repenting and crying until I spoke what the Holy Spirit told me to speak.

Jeremiah 20:9
But his word was in mine heart as a burning fire
shut up in my bones.

If you are under a spiritual leader that don't walk in the five fold ministry gifts, and you have a prophetic call on your life, you will **spiritually die!!!!**

Ephesians 4:11
And he gave some apostles; and some prophets;
and some evangelist; and some pastors and teachers.

A lot of ministries are centered on one person behind the pulpit doing everything. If anyone else has a teaching or evangelistic call, the pastor will only allow them to speak at certain times. What we call church is really sad today. People who walk in a prophetic calling in this day are called crazy. Prophets and prophetess are put down and told there are no more prophets. They even say there are no more apostles and speaking in tongues have ceased. I hear this all the time, when the Bible specifically says that these offices are in the body of Christ for the equipping of the saints. Matthew 5:17 says, "Think not that I am come to destroy the law, or **prophets**: I am not come to destroy, but to fulfill." This is written in red, which means Christ has said it Himself. It is very important to know who you are so that you don't let nobody put you in position that you were not chosen for.

2 Peter 1:10
Wherefore the rather, brethren, give diligence to make your calling and election sure: for if ye do these things, ye shall never fall:

There is a lot of misunderstandings, loneliness, and long suffering in a prophetic walk. A true prophet will not compromise. He or she loves what God love and hates what he hates. Prophets and prophetess see things others may not see.

In the Old Testament as I was studying about the prophets, the people hated to see them coming. As I begun to walk in prophetic calling, I could sense the coldness amongst the people when I walk in the room. Even in some buildings people call churches, the people would look at me as to say what is she going to say now. But I understand why some people and churches do not want a true prophet in their midst. People like to hear you prophesy house, money, and cars. Real prophets call out, repent and turn away from your sins. These are the last days and God is calling the church back to their first love.

The real meaning of church is ekklesia in Greek. The church is the called out ones, the ones called out from the world unto God. In simple form, the body of Christ.

Jeremiah 1:17 NKJV
Therefore prepare yourself and arise, And speak to them all that I command you. Do not be dismayed at their faces, Lest I dismay before them.

Many times in ministry leaders tend to get jealous if they see a person walking in gifting and callings and instead of training and teaching them, they cut them down and throw them out. In some cases, that is the best thing that can happen to you. We as people get complacent and comfortable. What seems like a bad thing could be a blessing. It was a blessing for me. I didn't have anyone to teach, train, and help me in the prophetic ministry. The local temples in my area do not know anything about the prophetic gift. My husband, who has a call on his life also, fasted and prayed with me that the Lord would open a door and lead us to someone or somewhere that could help us in our deliverance ministry. It is sad to say, but a lot of teachings we received was from some very anointed teachers off social media.

I am growing and walking in the gift that I was chosen to walk in. My husband is a big help in my spiritual growth. He is an awesome teacher, leader, and head.

THE CRY

In 2013, the Holy Spirit led me to start a woman's ministry. I did not know where to start or what to do. One day I was outside working in my yard and the Holy Spirit spoke to me and said Women Ablazed. Well, I walked inside and looked up ablaze. Wow, He said that the women that is a part of this group will walk in the same gifting and anointing I walk in. I am to train, teach and equip them for the ministry. These women will be blazed up in the fire of the Holy Ghost. Wow, that was shouting time for me. When God give you an assignment, look for the Devil. It seemed like doors slammed in face, The women did not want to talk to me. Instead of pulling toward me, they backed off. There were no communication, no money to do anything for the ministry, and spiritual attacks came from every position. Nothing went right. No matter how hard I prayed, it seemed as though God was not there. It was hard to even get in the presence of God. I felt like I was spiritually drained. I couldn't find nobody to help nor talk to. I know now why. The Lord had it fixed that way. I had to totally trust Him and Him alone. I had to keep pressing my way through prayer, fasting and studying. I fought hard everyday. He was preparing me for what is about to come on this earth in these last days. You will never be able to help anyone if you have never had to trust God in the midst of your storms. And a prophet and prophetess have to be totally delivered from walking in their feelings. I don't care who says what about me or to me. I come in the name of Jesus Christ of Nazareth. It is not about me! No matter, what is looks like or feel like. I walk by faith and not by sight, 2 Corinthians 5:7. I stand on the promises of God.

I find myself getting up early in the morning everyday crying and weeping for souls. My heart is so heavy with the intercessory prayer. Some days, I am physically drained in my body. It take days of rest and refills of praying, studying the word of God, and another baptism in the Holy Spirit. The devil wants to kill, steal, and destroy the women of God. As long as I have breath in my body, I will fight in the Spirit of the Holy Ghost.

TESTIMONY OF GOD'S AMAZING GRACE

THE BEGINNING OF LIFE

My entry into this world was difficult and untimely to say the least, heart felt. I entered this world as a seven month preemie. My mother told me she took a full bottle of aspirin, trying to abort me. The reasons for her action was quite overwhelming. She was only seventeen, still in high school, and my father denied his paternity. This pregnancy had all the makings of tragedy; teenage pregnancy, high school drop out, jobless, and no support from a father. But after the failed abortion, my mother said she felt so bad, because she realized that I was a life. Coming into this world weighing three pounds, I spent the first three months in a incubator. The doctor told my mother that my heart and lungs were severely undeveloped and I may not live.

At the age of seven, I was repeatedly molested by a relative. I was told if I ever told anyone, they would not believe me and would label me as a liar The damage from this abuse, felt like a jagged dagger piercing my very soul. The hurt was painful inside until I grew up hating men. I was not a lesbian, but when it came to men or sex, I was afraid. This prevented me from knowing true love.

At the age of nine I was in a wreck. My mother was driving her boyfriend's truck, with my cousin and me inside. A car pulled out in front of us but my mother could not stop. No one was hurt, but I I hit the floor and busted my right knee. The devil began to speak to my mind. He told me that no one loved me, I was black and ugly, and that I was better off dead.

The devil tried so many times to kill me. When I was about fifteen, I was driving my mother's car and I heard a lot of screeching tires and loud laughing. When I looked up, a car was doing donuts in the street and hit me head on. I could literally feel myself being picked up by force, that I later realized was an angel. My door swung open and I was thrown out of the car onto the ground. The car that hit

me, flipped in a ditch and one of the passengers was automatically killed. The only injury I sustained, once again, was a busted right knee.

Psalms 91:11
"For He will command His angels concerning you to guard you in all your ways."

I began to feel like I had a death wish on my life. Not knowing then, what I know now, it was not a death wish but a death angel. But no matter what the devil sent my way trying kill me, the Lord Almighty always guarded me with His Blood.

Isaiah 54:17
"No weapon that is fashioned against you shall succeed."

From the time I could remember as a child, I have always wondered why I was born. My life seemed so disappointing. I was physically and mentally abused from a close relative that always called me black, stupid, and ugly. I begin to believe the lies and really hated myself and the fact that I was dark-skinned. I would scrub my face with S.O.S pads, trying to remove the black color from my skin. Blood would run down my face from scrubbing it so hard.

I grew up in a family who really did not know how to show love. My mother did the best she could. She was a single parent and trying to raise three children. I was not brought up in a God-fearing family. Sure, we went to church services every once in a while. But what is the purpose of going to service and still live a willful sinful life? I would go to service with my aunt, but I still lived a sinful lifestyle.

I always felt like a outcast. I did not fit in with the in crowd. I tried the clubs, drinking, partying, and even dating. That lifestyle for me did not last long. I did not want to go to clubs or have premarital sex. But I found myself wrapped up in sin and all of its lustful pitfalls. My mind was so tormented and my heart ached with pain. All I wanted was true love. I did not think any one could love someone like me. The opinion that I had of myself was toxic. I felt so ugly and believed that I deserved to be treated badly. Everyday my life got worse and worse. I hated waking up to see another day. I began taking Tylenol P.M., trying t sleep my pain away. I would take up to seven pills a night. By the grace of God, I never overdosed or had any physical damage to my body. The Lord protected me even in my mess. I was having unprotected sex and never caught a STD or got pregnant. My life was miserable. I was smiling on the outside, but crying out for **HELP** on the inside.

NEW LIFE IN CHRIST

One night, I was in the act of committing fornication and my stomach begin to feel so queasy. I was literally getting sick to my stomach. I felt so bad. I knew that I could no longer live my life this way. The tugging at my heart from the Lord began that day. God was calling me to be holy and pure. I no longer wanted to live my life that way. But I could not help myself. One thing we must understand is when you are intimate with a person, your spirits become connected. That's why God ordained marriage. I had to be delivered from all those spirits that entered my temple through fornication. I wanted to be clean, delivered, and holy. My desire was for God to bless me with a man He had for me and not to take excess baggage into my holy matrimony.

After having a made up mind of wanting a better life, things began to change I was at a New ears Eve service and a young man pointed me out and began to speak to me things that only God and I knew. I felt the presence of God so heavy. I began to cry and weep before the Lord. The next week, the voice of the Lord spoke to me in my house. He told me that He loved me and He chose me and He chose me form my mother's womb to be a mouthpiece for Him. He showed me a vision of how the devil had tried to kill me, but he could not. Because the Lord had a purpose and plan for my life. I began to cry and repent. The following Sunday, I eagerly went to the temple in expectation of something great. That Sunday I was baptized and filled with the Precious Gift of the Holy Ghost. My life has never been the same.

As time went on, even though I was saved and filled with the Holy Ghost, there was still areas in my life that I needed to be healed and delivered from. The bitter roots of anger and the collection of excruciating pain and hurt still lived in me. There were many people who hurt me deeply and I had to forgive them in order to grow in the Lord. You must be honest and admit that you have hatred, bitterness or unforgiveness in your heart. I wanted to love those who hurt me with godly love and not just say it, but really mean it from the bottom of my heart. It wasn't easy for me. I cried out to the Lord and asked Him to help me.

We will never get anywhere in our ministry if we allow spirits of the enemy to manifest in our hearts. We must want deliverance in order to receive it. The devil intended to kill, steal, and destroy my ministry as well as my life, but God wouldn't allow it. All I have known growing up was pain and suffering, even in the temple. As a young woman in ministry, I have encountered a lot of put downs, misunderstandings and being lied on. But my ministry walk have been totally dependent on the Holy Ghost and not man! I have a love for hurting women because of my own experiences. This one thing I know for sure, the blood of Jesus can heal any wound and contrite spirit.

In July 2001, the Lord led my husband and I back to Mississippi from Illinois. Shortly afterward, I found out that I was pregnant. I was very excited. It was my first pregnancy and I have a love for children. When I went for my first check-up, I started to bleed very heavy. I went to the emergency room and the doctor sent me back home and told me to prop my feet up. I tried that, but the bleeding got heavier and I was in a lot of pain. My husband took me back to the ER In the city of Jackson, Ms which is about one hour and ten minutes away. I lost much blood and could not walk.

Once we made it to the ER in Jackson, I lost the activity of my limbs and I could not talk nor move. My vision had left. All I saw was black. I was praying in my heart as tears ran down my face. I felt like I was dying. The doctor said if I had not come when I did, I would have hemorrhaged to death. The doctors begin to prepare me for a blood transfusion. I started meditating on the Word of God in my heart, still unable to speak. My mother grabbed my hand and she prayed. Immediately my vision came back, strength came into my body and I sat up and began to praise the Lord. When the doctor checked my blood count it was normal. I did not have to have a transfusion. The enemy fought my mind with the feeling that I could not have children. But I believed that one day I would. I asked the Lord to bless my womb. I got pregnant three years after the miscarriage. I did not quit praying and believing. I now have a beautiful daughter name Jakeria.

TRUSTING CHRIST DESPITE LIFE'S TRIALS

In 2003, my mom was diagnosed with breast cancer. This was a very devastating thing to me. My mom and I were very close. My mom smiled when the doctor told her she had cancer. He was very rude telling her. He told her she was going to die in about three months. My mother was hurt, but she was a very strong woman. She said I am going to fight. I am not going to just take this sitting down. I am very strong faith believer in the Lord Almighty.

So my mother was not going to be fighting, praying and believing by herself. At the time my baby was and infant and I was really wanting to stay at home and spend as much time with her as I could. But unfortunately, my mother had to start chemotherapy and radiation everyday for sex weeks. Well, I had to drive her to Jackson, MS. My husband was employed and we only had one vehicle. I had to take him to work which was about seventeen miles away each morning at five thirty. After dropping him off at work I had to then come back home and pick my mother up and take her for treatments. I had to carry my infant baby in the infectious hospital everyday. My body was worn out!!!!!!!!!! After retiring home each evening, I still did my house chores and cooked each day for my family.

My mother's cancer had left for about three months and then it came back and it had spread all over her body even to her brain. She had started to forget. She had memory shortage. It was time to move momma in with me I knew she could no longer take care of herself. It was very hard for me to see my mother like this. The chemotherapy had paralyzed her from the waist down. I had to take total care of momma. And all the time, I had a small child and husband to be there for.

I found out I was pregnant again and I was really sick everyday, but I had to take care of momma, I had nurses to come in but once the nurses leave, I am on my own to change her, turn her, and feed her. One day, I was feeling a little cramping in my stomach, and I went to the restroom, and all of a sudden, my baby came out in the toilet. He was attached to the umbilical cord. I was fifteen weeks pregnant.

I remember sitting there screaming and crying. I called out to my husband and he came and got me to the floor and wrapped our son in a towel. He then called the ambulance. My cousin had to come and get my mom and take her to my grandmother's house until I got out of the hospital. I was hurt because my husband and I wanted a son so dearly. Afterward, my husband picked my mother up and took both of us back home. I could not take the pain pills the doctor prescribed because they it would have made me very drowsy. I could not sleep all day. Who was going to take care of momma? I was in so much pain, all I could do was cry. I could barely walk, but I still took care of my mom.

I started feeling a little better. About five months later, I started to feel sick once again. I went to the doctor and found out I was pregnant. I was so happy. I still was thinking about having to take care of my mother with no help!!! I was not able to go anywhere and leave momma alone. I missed the weekend outings with my husband and daughter. I practically gave up my entire life and my family's for my mother. Thank God for a loving and understandable husband who helped me and understood that I only have one mother who would have did the same for me. When I told my mother I was pregnant again, she smiled and she told me that she felt like I should put her in a nursing home. That was the last thing I wanted to hear. She told me that she loved me, and appreciated everything I had done for her, but she did not want me to loose another baby. I told her that I would pray about it. With much crying and praying I decided to put her in a nursing home. I would go to the nursing home everyday and stay with her. Everyday, I still made sure that my house was clean and I had a cook meal for my family. I hated seeing my mother lying in the bed slowly dying.

My mother died December 11, 2009. It felt like a part of me died along with her. Once mother dies you can no longer hear her voice, touch her, or kiss her. Eve though my mother died, I could not allow myself to shut down, I still have a husband and daughter who needs me. Each day, I cried an prayed for the Lord to keep my mind.

Isaiah 26:3
"You will keep him in perfect peace, whose mind is stayed on YOU, because he trusts in You."

I had a doctor's appointment January 26, 2010. I was concerned about this appointment because I had noticed a small amount of cramping in my abdomen. I know its normal as the baby grow, but with ml previous miscarriages, I was very careful about the least pain. When I went for my check-up, the doctor liked at me and said, "Mrs Williams I have bad news." I said I already know. What is the problem this time? He said, "You have dilated three centimeters and I can see the baby and the bag. In other words, this baby is coming out very soon and there is nothing we can do to stop him." The doctor gave two options. One option was to go into the hospital and they speed the process of my labor, or I can go back home until he comes out.

I began to cry. This was very overwhelming. I was five months pregnant. I knew that my baby was a boy. No doctor had to tell me. I felt it in my heart. I called my husband at work and told him what was going on, he was so hurt. I could hear it in his voice. We decided to go to another hospital to get a second opinion. When we arrived at the hospital, they checked me. The result was the same as the first. We decided to go ahead and speed up the process of labor. After my water broke, I started to get chills and high fever. I felt like I was dying. I could feel the baby kicking and moving inside of me. I was so hurt. I knew once he was delivered, he would not live. The doctors said his heart and lungs were not developed enough to live outside the womb. I started to set up an infection in my body because the baby was between my cervix and uterus.

The doctors was telling me to push. If I did not get the baby out soon, I was going to die of an infection. After about five pushes, he came out and the doctor immediately started antibiotics. The nurse took my son to clean him up, and she brought him back for my husband and I to hold him. That was very hard for me to do. Holding my tiny son in my arms, and he was dead. My husband was so hurt over not only losing yet again another son but seeing me go through so much hurt and pain. He said he is thankful to the Lord that I am still living and well.

All these tragedies happened to me in such a short period of time. I felt like just giving up on everything. A part of me could not give up no matter what happened. I still love the Lord God Almighty with all my heart, soul, and mind. I just want His will to be done in my life.

Job 13:15
"Though He slay me, yet will I trust Him."

I know everything happened in my life for a reason. I may not understand, but I trust the Lord enough to know that everything will be all right. There is no stopping me!!!!!!!!!!!!!!!!

To God Be The Glory!!!!!!!!!

GOD'S DIVINE ORDER

ORDER OF MANKIND

And the Lord God said, "It is not good that man should b alone; I will make him a helper comparable to him," Genesis 2:18 (NKJV). A helper is someone that helps in getting or doing something. A woman was made to be a helper to a man. Women are to help their husbands in whatever area he needs assistance in as ling as it is something that does not goes against scripture. Being a helper does not mean, in any way, women are inferior. Women have a particular place and role in this life. We should fill our role and walk in it. We should not argue with God's divine order. After all, God made us a woman and that is what He intended for us to be.

"And He answered and said to them, 'Have you not read that he who made them at the beginning made them male and female,' and said, 'For this reason a man shall leave his father and mother and be joined to his wife, and the two shall become one flesh? So then, they are no longer two but one flesh. Therefore what God has joined together, let no man separate," Matthew 19:4-6 (NKJV). When a woman marries a man, they become one flesh. No one should be able o come between the bond that they share. The man does not just leave his father and mother, but the wife should, also. Most women have a big problem with this. "But I want you to know that the head of every man is Christ, the head of woman is man, and the head of Christ is God," 1 Corinthians 11:3 (NKJV). When women refuse to follow this order, they no longer have a problem with man but God. The man did not make the order, God did. The order of God does not change for **no one.** Whatever God says, that seals it. If we don't obey the Word of God, then we will suffer the consequences.

PERSONAL TESTIMONY OF MARRIAGE AND SUBMISSION

He who finds a wife finds a good thing and obtain favor from the Lord, Proverbs 18:22 (NKJV).

In November 2000, the Lord blessed me to meet the man of God He had preserved just for me. Three months before I met my husband, the Lord gave me a dream of me in a wedding gown and I saw a light-complexioned hand in mine. I never saw a face. When I met my husband and shook his hand, I felt a very strong connection that I had never felt before. He told me he was moving the next week to Rockford, Ill. He said the Lord spoke to him and said I was his wife. I knew deep within that I was. I prayed and asked the Lord to show me if he was my husband. I had the same dream, but this time I saw my husband's face. He move to Illinois and I stayed in Mississippi where I was attending a community college. We communicated by phone for the three months. In March 2001, I moved to Rockford and we married.

Many marriages today fail simply because women are not teaching their daughters or other women how to love thee husband and children Titus 2:3-5 (NKJV) says that older women are to be reverent in behavior, not slanderers, not given to much wine, teachers of good things; that they teach the young women to love their husbands and their children, to be discreet (self controlled), chaste (pure), homemakers (workers at home), good(kind), **obedient (submissive)** to their own husbands, that the Word of God may not be blasphemed (reviled or spoke about in a very critical or resulting way).

Submission is obedience or yield to the control or power of another. The word submission is such a hard word for women in this century. But it is such a blessing if women submit unto their husbands. Ephesians 5:22 (NKJV) says wives should submit to their own husbands as unto the Lord. 1 Peter 3:7 (NKJV) mentions that the husbands, likewise, live with their wives in a understanding way, showing honor to the woman as the weaker vessel, since they are heirs with you of the grace of life, so that your prayers may not be hindered. This verse doesn't only apply to the husband. It applies to the wife, also. If the wife is not submissive, then she is out of order and her prayers will be hindered. I know from experience.

Coming from a single parent home and being the only girl with two brothers and no father in my life, there were many struggles. For most of my childhood years, my mom had a man in the house that was not her husband. I never had a relationship with my father. Being that I was repeatedly molested by a relative and told not to tell anyone, I grew up hating men. I did not have a godly example of marriage nor how to be submissive to authority.

When I got saved and filled with the Holy Ghost, He began to transform my mind, heart soul and body. So, I fasted and prayed that the Lord will deliver me from the bitterness that I had carried so long. I longed then for a husband, a companion, a soul mate, and a best friend. The Lord delivered me and blessed me with my husband. Then the submission process began. One morning when my husband was leaving for work, I had a snappy attitude before he left. I got on my knees to pray and the Holy Spirit spoke to me and said, "Daughter, there is no need for you to talk to me. You must repent to your husband and then I will hear you." I could not wait until my husband called me on is lunch break. I immediately responded to what God told me to do and asked for my husband's forgiveness. I needed to pray to my Father and I did not want my prayers hindered.

Submission is a wife's choice. No one can do it for her. No one can make her do it. Do you know the main reason why wives do not submit to their husbands? They are afraid of what will happen if their husbands do things his way instead of their way. A marriage

Personal Testimony Of Marriage And Submission

---

will not work if there are two heads. Ephesians 5:23-24 (NKJV) says for the husband is the head of the wife, as also Christ is the head of the church; and He is the Savior of the body. Therefore just as the church is subject to Christ, so let the wives subject to their own husbands in everything.

The devil lie and tells women they can have it all. That is not what the Word of God says. It is very selfish for a woman to get married and have a child or children and think only about what she wants and the things she never had a chance to do in the world. The world makes being a godly wife and mother such a terrible thing. The Word of God tells us that we are to be workers at home. If your children and husband are lacking in any area, then the wife is out of the will of God. So, if you are not a woman willing to submit to proper spiritual authority and covering, you are not ready for marriage. God calls man to be the head of the home and the provider.

THE ORDER OF GOD

*I*n society today, day cares and the Boys and Girls Club have become parents because some women have allowed their careers and their dreams to be more important than raising a family. In most homes, women are the sole providers. We have allowed sin to come in and strayed away from the Word of God. God never intended women to work eight or nine hours a day and then maintain a home. When we allow Satan to keep us too occupied with our careers and chasing our dreams, our homes become neglected. Once you have children, it is all about them until they are of the age to take care of themselves.

Submission to the order of God's word will bring blessings and the favor of God in your life. God has an order, and when we get out of His order, we open our spirit up or demonic attacks. Satan has attacked and defeated marriages and families. The body of Christ must walk in the power of the Holy Ghost to get God's Order back into the home and church, the called out ones. The church has gotten away from the Word of God and it has caused many divorces and curses on the family. Women, today, do not fear God and take heed of His voice. It is a blessing to stay under proper headship authority. God set up authority for a reason. When we do not obey it, it causes terrible consequences. Many times women are so quick to speak and not think about the consequences of their words. We need to pray and ask the Holy Spirit to bridle our tongue. I'm so grateful and appreciative to the Lord for the order He has ordained. Wives are to pray for their husbands. Proverbs 21:9 says it is better to live in a corner of a housetop, than in a house shared with a contentious woman. We feel as though we have to be heard and everything have to be our way or we are not satisfied. Some women even use control over their husbands and hold back sex if he does not do what she wants. That is witchcraft. At that point, women, you have become a witch. Anytime a person uses control or mind manipulation on a person to get what they want, it is WITCHCRAFT.

We should keep our priorities in order daily. God should always be first in our daily lives. We should have a life of dedication of fasting and praying. Being a wife and mother takes a disciplined mind and will. You have to give up your selfish will and put your husband and children before yourself. Marriage and family is the representation of Christ and the Church. When you are born again, you give up your will for God's will. If we keep our priorities in order, then we will be blessed beyond measure.

Lashanda S. Williams is a woman after God's heart and determined to fulfill the will of her Father. Her heart is to reach lost, dying souls and direct them to the only help, Jesus Christ. Lashanda has been chosen by God to proclaim the Gospel of Jesus Christ. She loves God and her family. She is married to Jake P. Williams and have one daughter name Jakeria S. Williams. Lashanda lives what she preaches an teaches. She encourages women in the Lord, giving all glory and honor unto her Lord. She prays by her testimony of God's saving grace and her experiences, that each woman that reads this book will experience true deliverance just as she has. When things seem impossible, know that all things are possible with God.

My grace is sufficient for thee: for my strength is made perfect in weakness......2 Corinthians 12:9 (KJV)

If the Son therefore shall make you free, ye shall be free indeed..........John 8:36 (KJV)

And know that all things work together for good to them that love God, to them who are the called according to his purpose..........Romans 8:28 (KJV)

www.ingramcontent.com/pod-product-compliance
Ingram Content Group UK Ltd.
Pitfield, Milton Keynes, MK11 3LW, UK
UKHW041957230426
12048UKWH00008B/383